3 Steps to
Successful Salary Negotiation

Bri Jones

Copyright © 2019 Bri Jones

All rights reserved. No part of this publication may be reproduced, stored in a retrieved system, or transmitted, in any form or by any means, electronic, mechanical, photocopying, recording, or otherwise, except for the inclusion of brief questions in a review, without prior permission in writing from the author.

Library of Congress Cataloging-in-Publication Data

1-7539635068

ISBN-10: 0-9964702-7-1

ISBN-13: 978-0-9964702-7-8

DEDICATION

This is for the Ambitious Women who are ready to conquer the obstacles, challenges and discriminations that try to stand in their way. Never give up, never settle. You are enough. Claim what you deserve!

Contents

    Acknowledgments

1   Introduction

2   Stigma of Negotiation

3   Why and When should you Negotiate?

4   Preparing for Salary Negotiation

5   What to consider for Salary Negotiation

6   Highlighting the value of your Attributes

7   Negotiating with Finesse

8   When to Accept or Decline a Salary Offer

9   Effectively request for a Salary Increase

    Message from the Author

Acknowledgments

I give acknowledgement and thanks to God for always providing for my family and blessing me with favor. I want to acknowledge my son, family and friends for their continuous support, prayers and encouragement. Thank you to my readers. My sincere gratitude to my supporters, I am internally grateful.

Introduction

Women are often powerhouses in corporate environments. We have come a long way from being the silent partner in running our households to being the breadwinners or valued partners in the many households. Women are not just playing supporting roles in the workplace, they are the leaders of major industries. Women such as media proprietor and philanthropist Oprah Winfrey; Ursula Burns, who worked her way up the ranks in 28 years to the role of CEO of the Fortune 500 company Xerox; Ginni Rometty, the first woman to lead IBM as Chairman, President and CEO; and Sheila Johnson, BET cofounder, CEO of Salamanders Hotel and Resorts and stake owner of several professional sports teams, are businesswomen proving that women know how to lead. With many women in superior roles why are so many women still getting the superior or equivalent pay as men doing the same job? According to a recent study by the Institute for Women's Policy Research, women average 80 percent of a man's salary, resulting in the high gender pay gap. Case studies show that one reason for this imbalance is that women are not engaging in salary negotiation when it comes to accepting new employment.

I maintain many roles in the corporate world as a financial consultant, author, mentor and speaker. I have been in the financial industry collectively for more than 18 years. I enjoy the fact that I never stop learning. I am passionate about sharing my experience and knowledge with others to aid in their success. I have mentored numerous women in salary negotiation and many other topics. I was inspired to write this book because of this negligence in the meaning and understanding of salary negotiation versus the typical negotiation we do in our daily lives. Negotiation is defined as a method to overcome an obstacle or difficult path through discussion.

The solution is to bridge the gap of consciousness and implementation of salary negotiation. When you finish reading this book you will have the tools to confidently prepare for salary negotiation, know what to consider when negotiating your salary, be able to highlight your attributes to increase your value with a new employer, know when to accept or decline a salary offer and as a bonus, have learned how to effectively request for a salary increase.

STIGMA OF NEGOTIATION

There is a belief that when offered a job, one should be grateful and accept the offer first provided by an employer. There is a stigma associated with asking for more monetary compensation. That is often driven by lack of knowledge and fear of conflict with an employer. However, several studies show that when one attempts to strategically negotiate a desirable salary, there is a more favorable result for the employee. One reason for the gender pay gap that finds women earning 80 percent less than men, may be women's unwillingness and fear of salary negotiation. We are going to discuss the key methods of improving preparation, awareness, confidence and the approach to achieving success in salary negotiation.

The goal is to stop leaving money on the table and confidently reclaim the value of your time and significance you bring to an employer. Women who practice salary negotiation have a 20 percent chance, or higher, of increasing their salaries.

The purpose of salary negotiation is for the employer and employee to come to a WIN/WIN agreement. Allowing the employer to understand the value and asset the employee is willing to contribute to the business. In addition, the employee is expected to deliver satisfactory performance and engagement. Salary negotiation reestablishes the employee's confidence and improves the ability to advance financially faster starting with the initial salary agreement. When women do not engage in salary negotiation, they limit their opportunities to advance their financial growth. It will seem as though seeking employment with another company is the only way to receive a significant increase in pay. Securing a strategic salary negotiation skill enables women to possess a more gratifying earning and reduce the high gender pay gap.

Have you ever made a purchase from a classified advertising company, similar to Craigslist, or even bought items at a flea market? What was your interaction when you were conducting the transaction? Did you pay the price listed? Did you counter offer a lower price?

Have you ever purchased a vehicle or accompanied someone purchasing a vehicle? When you were at the dealership, did you volunteer to pay the listed price on the vehicle? Did you try to pull teeth to get the best reduced price out of the sales person? With the mindset, if they don't give you the offer you want, you will decline and leave.

Lastly, have you ever taken advantage of the "price match" system in stores such as Target, Walmart or BestBuy? When you're shopping at a store that offers price match and you know the competitor is offering additional savings, what do you do? Do you pay for your product without inquiring about the additional savings, or do you encourage the cashier to apply the price match savings?

I think you can agree that you have experienced one of those transactions at some point in your life. I want you to take a brief moment and think about those transactions.

Now, that I have you thinking about your daily interactions with negotiation, I want you to think about how you approach the conversation of *Your Salary, Your Livelihood* and *Your Way Of Living* for you and your family. Do you handle it the same way as saving a few dollars here and there? You are probably saying no, just like I was several years ago.

My friends used to tease me and call me a New Yorker, because I negotiated everything from flea market items to name brands at major department stores in the mall. However, there was one place I never attempted to negotiate and that was at work.

When I started my career, no one ever told or taught me how to negotiate my salary or even advised me that it was open for discussion. This was something I had to learn over time with trial and error and a lot of research. I always knew there was a discriminating bias in gender pay, but I didn't realize I was part of that problem. I was under the false impression that my education and experience would get me a sensible salary. How could I truly expect to get something if I never asked?

It wasn't until my early 30s that I reached a point in my career where I wanted more. I acknowledged my worth and what I brought to the table. I was tired of feeling like I had to reenter the job market to seek a higher salary, because the little annual merit employers were giving just didn't cut it. I found myself looking for a new job almost annually, because I didn't set my salary foundation correctly when I accepted a job opportunity. I was dramatically behind the salary average for my field, industry and area. I couldn't be upset with anyone but myself.

If you are able to relate, keep reading. There's more

treasure in store for you!

After I started doing my research I learned most employers' first offer ranged from 2 to 8 percent less than what they were willing to pay in salary to a new employee.

Think about how many job offers you accepted without negotiating your salary? How many times did you leave money on the table for the employer to keep in their pockets without you blinking an eye?

During the life of our professional career from start to retirement, if we never negotiate, we are depriving our income by thousands of dollars each time we accept a new job.

I want you to really think about that and let it sink in. The average person is in the work force for more than 40 years. Most enter their professional career in their mid-20s. We could be giving away between $1 million and $1.5 million in the life of our professional career! (Economist Linda Babcock of Carnegie Mellon University)

Are you knowingly, willing and able to give away a million dollars to a multi-million or multi-billion-dollar company? I am not. That's truly disturbing to me. I'm just not that generous to give a company already making millions and billions of dollars off my labor and talent any additional funds. Not even a thousand dollars if I can help it.

It was unfortunate for me that I was so far behind the salary market average, but I had enough. I refused to settle for less anymore! I did my research, created my plan and practiced. I built my confidence and most of all, I obtained multiple career offers at the same time.

When I strengthened my knowledge about salary negotiation, I was able to increase my salary by more than 48 percent from leaving one employer to the next. This salary increase did not include the value of the benefits package. You can just image how far behind the salary market average I was, but I made a comeback by applying my research and knowledge.

Can you image if I would have done that just 5 to 10 years ago? I gave away a minimum of $250,000 by my lack of knowledge in salary negotiation. This figure was determined based on the salary average in my field versus my salary and the difference per year I didn't negotiate.

I presume as you're reading this the lightbulb is shining even brighter, and the enthusiasm is starting to form bigger inside your belly.

There is no reason why we should not be properly compensated for our talents, hard work and value that we bring to an organization.

It starts with US!

WHY AND WHEN SHOULD YOU NEGOTIATE?

We should exhibit negotiation practices daily, whether it is to obtain more savings or add additional income to our paycheck. Yes, salary negotiation can be intimidating for some women, but it is one of the most significant, demanding discussions to have at the foundation of your professional career. Women are able to negotiate; we just don't implement our skills as consistently for ourselves as we do when we are representing someone else. Many women are commonly considered scholars at negotiating for savings on small or major purchases, fundraising, or getting our children or family out of trouble. Women also strive in negotiating on behalf of clients and businesses. Most women won't consider settling for less than what they deem acceptable. Women will deploy a go-getter methodology until the desired outcome is achieved. Women will display strength, confidence and drive when negotiating on another's behalf. However, for some reason, when it comes to their own salaries, some women are willing to settle for the first offer or "no" response.

Achieving the objective of remaining in control of the negotiation conversation starts with avoiding salary discussions until after you receive an official job offer. The ability to redirect a salary request before an offer letter is presented is an important skill to master. You want potential employers to invest time in you with multiple interview sessions, acknowledge that they need you and start envisioning you as part of their team. Redirecting or delaying the conversation until the rapport is established is important. However, you never want to completely disregard the salary request from the employer. Disregarding the salary request could be misinterpreted as noncompliance. Attempt to get the employer to give the first number. You do not want to offer the first number because it could underbid or overbid yourself out of consideration for the position.

You need to consistently practice salary negotiation, which can take place any time during the interviewing process. Preparation is key. Before the initial interview, take the time to organize your negotiation points and be able to provide relevant supporting information. Supporting information can be found on Payscale.com, Glassdoor and Google. Maximizing your salary is knowing the facts about the relevant market's assessment of the specific profession and incorporating how your unique skills lines up with the employers' requirements.

When asked to provide your salary request, attempt redirecting the question to the employer. Always demonstrate genuine interest. Acknowledge the employer's request with a response such as;

- *I was hoping to learn more about the daily task and demands of this role before discussing salary.*
- *I'm sure we can come to an agreement that would be in the best interest of the organization and myself.*
- *Do you mind telling me the salary range or what the budget is for this position?*
- *I am willing to consider any reasonable salary offer.*
- *What do you feel a candidate with my experience and education is worth to this organization?*

If the employer is adamant about giving a salary answer, provide one. You should base your response on your research and your needs, but be realistic. Don't undervalue or overstate yourself. Give a small range within $5,000 to $10,000. Your lowest number should be the minimum amount you are willing to accept. Be honest with yourself. You don't want to waste your time if the employer cannot meet your minimum requirement. So, if you are willing to accept a minimum of $50,000/year, then you should respond with a salary range of $50,000 to $60,000. If you are advancing your career, you should request at least a 15 percent increase of your previous salary — this is only if you were already at market rate. If you are applying for a lateral position, you should request at least a 5 percent increase from your previous salary if you are already at market rate. If you were not at market rate, you should request for a salary at market rate average that is supported by your experience and education. As we get further along, we will discuss the tactics for finding an accurate salary figure.

Negotiation is not limited to employment situations. It should be incorporated in every transaction or interaction where money is exchanged for goods and services. If you are a contractor, an artist or entrepreneur, you should be negotiating your compensation for the goods and services you provide. Research and be familiar with the market rates and competitors in your specific industry. Unfortunately, some will waste years accepting the bare minimum because they are afraid of losing the opportunity. We have to stay competitive in the industry to remain financially stable. We will start negotiating when we are ready to create solutions that will produce new results, but don't lose too much time procrastinating. We have to be mentally ready for better.

But who is actually playing the game?

I surveyed 80 men and women from the ages of 25 to 60. I asked participants to recall when or if they ever negotiated their salaries. The survey consisted of the following questions: At what age did the participant start negotiating their salary? What inspired the participant to initiate salary negotiation?

Unfortunately, my results were not surprising. Seventy percent of women ages 25 to 34 were not negotiating their salaries. Of women ages 35 and older, 45 percent practiced salary negotiation, while 55 percent never negotiated their salary. Men ages 25 to 34 were 65 percent more likely to negotiate their salary. While 80 percent of men ages 35 and older negotiated their salaries.

The reasons varied for the participants who did not negotiate. The answers revealed that it was due to government pay grade restrictions, contract budgeting limits or not having the courage or knowledge to negotiate, in addition to fear of rejection and the fear of sabotaging the relationship with a potential new employer. There was more consistency in the justification to negotiate. The answers conveyed that the participants understood their value, received encouragement from family members, guidance from mentors and benefitted from their research and life experience.

PREPARING FOR SALARY NEGOTIATION

I can't stress it enough: Salary negotiation is a critical skill to develop if you want to advance financially. Plan, research and practice are the three key factors you execute before meeting with a prospective employer. Interviewing and salary negotiating is stressful enough for some, so you don't want to create additional challenges by not being prepared. Mental preparation affects your body language. Nonverbal language can convey as much or more than verbal. The goal is to demonstrate confidence and security. The more prepared you are, the smoother the interaction and results will be. Most importantly before you apply for a position, make sure your resume reflects why you deserve the higher salary.

While life has taught us everything doesn't always go as planned, it's still important to map things out, which leaves us more conditioned, leading to a higher rate of success when the unexpected happens. Before you apply for a job, you should know the salary range, the minimum experience, education and certification requirements for the position. You don't want to waste your time interviewing for a job that doesn't meet your financial needs or invest the time applying for a job for which you don't qualify. Never go into an interview not knowing what your minimum salary requirement is. Identify what you need and want from your new employment.

- How much money do you need to be comfortable to pay all your bills, take care of yourself and your family, enjoy life and have balance?

- What type of work schedule adapts to your life balance and responsibilities?
- Do you want to work weekends, overtime or a nine to five? How much flexibility do you need from your employer?
- In what type of work environment are you the most productive?
- How well do you work in stressful and demanding environments?
- Are you flexible to work in a team or an individual environment?
- Are you looking for short-term or long-term employment?

These are some of the questions you should be asking yourself when categorizing the best job to apply for. You want to create a balance and be as happy as possible with your employer. If you have balance and are happy, then you will be more productive.

Create a prioritized list using the answers from the

questions presented in the previous paragraph as a start. This is structure in developing your negotiation goals. I strongly suggest not having an all or nothing approach to negotiation: Be flexible and willing to compromise where possible. You don't want to demonstrate an aggressive, conflicting or hard to work with attitude during an interview. That won't help you at all.

Don't get stuck in a box because of what you were previously paid. Don't allow new employers to base their offers on your salary history. Strategically, fight back! Don't lie about your salary history because the new employer can verify that. Don't become wary and decline to answer. Give a salary range of what you were paid. One technique I have used in the past when I was below the salary market value was giving the total of my annual salary and benefits package value as my annual compensation.

You can get the monetary value of your benefits package from your human resource department. Don't be afraid to express to the new employer that the concern is your current pay because your previous employment was not comparable to the current market.

You also have to be ready to display what you can offer your employer in return. Be prepared to prove your value through previous employment achievements and exposure. You want to emphasize what the employer will gain by hiring you. You can validate your salary request by being prepared to highlight your skills, experience, qualifications and accomplishments.

Time is money. Work smarter, not harder.

Research is a great tool to master to obtain a better understanding and knowledge of an employer, industry and career opportunity. The resources available to conduct research have changed a lot over decades. Now information is available to anyone with internet access. Even with that convenience, we still need to make sure we are retrieving information from trustworthy resources. There are several reliable websites to utilize when researching a specific job market, industry and employment. Websites such as Glassdoor, PayScale, Salary.com and Google are great resources to discover salary range for specific or similar jobs in a desired area. Websites like Indeed.com offer employee reviews, which are helpful in deciding if a company is fa good fit for you. Assess the positive and negative reviews. Be cautious because some employees may have ulterior motives or biases toward an organization. Visit the company's website to gather vital information about their financial status, history and career advancement opportunities. If you are looking for an employer you can grow with and invest your time in, this information is imperative. If a potential employer's financial condition is weak, you may be able to avoid the unexpected layoff due to insufficient cash flow available to support normal business operations. Sometimes the unforeseen downsizings cannot be foreseen, but if you do your due diligence you may save yourself the distress of unemployment again shortly after being hired.

It is a good idea to be familiar with the type of organization you are applying for. Is the employer for profit, nonprofit or a private sector? You want to know how the employer is accumulating income and how reliable are the resources. Be familiar with how long the company has been in business and their growth trends, especially if your plan is to stay long term. Know the competitors and the demand for the organization. Compare industries with similar demographics such as company size, profit, industry, location and professional title. Find out what the market says about the longevity of the industry.

Attend networking events to discover the best employers to work for, booming industries that are up and coming, and gain employment referral opportunities. In a lot of major industries, advancing your financial status is more about who you know than what you know. So, developing those business networking relationships is essential. You can also use those business relationships to gain knowledge on the salary demand for specific positions. Connect with people in your field. The best thing to do is get a mentor who has mastered or is on the path to where you want to be. Join social groups in your profession through social media. Learn from others' success and failures. Join your alma mater's alumni association. Don't be afraid to ask your peers what their plan of execution looks like. Although many people are not comfortable sharing specifics about their salary, they may be willing to share opinions on what a person with your experience and education level should expect to earn.

When researching your desired salary, consider your level of experience, education and the demand of the position in the desired area of the employer. A career opportunity in San Diego, California is not going to be the same as Pittsburgh, Pennsylvania. The cost of living is dramatically different. Therefore, employers understand to acquire good employees for high demanding roles they need to provide reasonable living compensation. However, you need to be fully equipped with the knowledge of your market value to an employer. Yes, it is important to research the employer, salary and other vital information, but it is equally imperative to do the research on your market value to the industry. Know and understand your worth before you go into an interview. Knowing your market value to an industry will help prevent you from under bidding or overbidding your salary request. Of course, you don't want to leave money on the table, but don't overbid yourself out of a job opportunity.

Practice makes perfect or at least makes you better. Planning and researching salary average, evaluating employers and analyzing your market value is vital, but practicing is a collective key to success. What good is investing time in planning and researching if you can't have a meaningful conversation without fumbling all over the place? You want to be knowledgeable, but you want to create a confident and clear dialogue.

There are no limits on the ways you can prepare for your interview and salary negotiation. Practice in the mirror, speaking out loud and maintaining eye contact with your reflection. This is a valuable technique to take note of your facial expressions and gestures you may want to avoid during the interview. Practice with a friend or associate and be open to their feedback. Constructive criticism is productive to improve your deficiencies. Rehearse redirecting salary discussion prior to official job offer and your salary negotiation approach. When practicing use different scenarios responses from the employer and attempt to problem solve the challenges. By the time you schedule your initial interview, you should have several practice sessions complete.

Keep your options open and interview for multiple meaningful positions. Don't waste your time on interviews for jobs you have no intention on accepting. When you are interviewing for multiple positions, save the best for last if possible. Learn from your mistakes beginning with the least favorable job interview. Take notes during and after the interview. Don't be afraid to ask the employer for feedback after your interview is complete. By the time you get to the last interview on your roster, you should be a professional.

What to Consider for Salary Negotiation

Always incorporate salary negotiation when the time arises. Never accept defeat at the first mention of rejection. Have the not-a-quitter attitude and be willing to put on your problem-solving hat and go to work. If an employer refuses to consider your counteroffer, don't surrender yet. Salaries can include base compensation, commission incentives and bonuses, such as signing, performance and annual. If more money is not a possibility, maintain your professional poker face and provide an alternative to the monetary salary. Yes, we all want to maximize our base salary to see our paychecks increase but, have you ever considered negotiating the benefits compensation? Employee benefits may not seem to have a direct effect on your paycheck, but when structured properly they create greater savings. That keeps more money in your pockets. Make sure to incorporate the all-inclusive monetary and benefits package when negotiating.

Many employers prefer negotiating benefits to providing more monetary compensation. Nonmonetary benefits are relatively low in cost to the employer, even though the benefits could result in higher savings for you. The employer could benefit greater at no cost, low cost and achieve higher tax deduction benefits. There are numerous benefits you can incorporate in salary negotiation that could create savings immediately or could benefit you in the future. Investing the time now to have those uncomfortable conversation could ultimately payoff in the future or in your next employment. Either way it's worth having the discussion.

Have you ever considered negotiating for a better job title? Obtaining a better job title can be a benefit for you when you begin looking for another job. If the job title is an accountant, depending on your job responsibilities, the employer may consider changing your title to senior accountant. If the job title is secretary, the employer may consider changing your title to executive assistant. Both of those job titles look very appealing on your resume going forward. However, if the employer rejects your request, counteroffer to consider the title change when you take on more responsibilities. Creating balance and fulfillment in the workplace is priceless. Weigh in on negotiating a guaranteed severance package contract. This will give you the extra security due to a decline in the economy or if the employer has an unforeseen financial hardship, bankruptcy or high layoffs. This is not at an immediate cost to the employer, but it will probably decrease the likelihood of you being laid off if there are alternatives. The key is to ask.

Consider requesting transportation allowance. Transportation allowance could include public transportation, taxi service, fuel reimbursement or parking garage costs. Employers commonly offer a percentage of transportation allowance for public transportation and garage parking in most major cities, but you could request for additional funds or complete reimbursement. Transportation allowance for the employee is a benefit to employers because it is a taxable deduction.

Incorporating professional development and tuition reimbursement in your benefits negotiation is a great future investment and savings to you. Advancing your education and knowledge at the employer's expense will directly create new opportunities for you. This could help you advance your career within the company and justify a larger annual increase during your performance review. This is also a tax benefit for the employer.

Consider negotiating a higher employer price match toward your retirement package after the probation period or ask for immediate employer price match on start date. This is your future investment, don't take it lightly. Don't forget to include additional paid time off to your negotiation list. One of my previous employers required each employee to take one paid personal day off every month. This was a use it or lose it method. This was to ensure focus, the mental stability and productivity in the success of the business. These factors added so much priceless value and balance to work, life and health. Mental rejuvenation is priceless. Mental, physical and emotional health can mean fewer doctors' bills and a healthier longer life!

I saved my favorite benefit to negotiate for last. Teleworking or also known as remote working! Teleworking provides so much flexibility, savings and relieves stress. The savings are immediate. Working from home saves on commuting expenses, gas costs and results in less wear and tear on your vehicle. I can really appreciate not sitting in traffic for over an hour to only drive 18 miles. There is no set formula to negotiating a specific schedule to work remotely. This depends on the demand of the job to have you on-site for meetings or physical availability. You can request for a set amount of days to work remotely during the week or month collectively or even negotiating teleworking on an as-needed bases. This is at no cost to the employer. However, you must demonstrate you are just as reliable out of the office as you would be in the office.

When negotiating for benefits, you don't want to overwhelm the employer with multiple benefit adjustments. This could become unappealing to the employer and not work in your favor. You need to determine what benefit items are most significant to you. Consider discussing two benefits that would make the most impact in your life and explain why those adjustments could be a WIN/WIN for both parties. For example, additional paid time off will ensure a rejuvenated approach toward work focus, productivity and dedication.

HOW TO HIGHLIGHT YOUR ATTRIBUTES

You cannot exclusively depend on the job description to harmonize with your capabilities. All employers have a set of additional desirable qualities that are considered when making the decision to hire a new employee. Unfortunately, employers don't normally volunteer that information to the candidates. It is up to you to retrieve that information from the employer and intently incorporate your qualities simultaneously with the employer's needs. The most common characteristics employers are looking for is good communication skills, leadership, customer service, adaptability and great work ethics. Some of these qualities you can demonstrate during the interview process. Good communication skills are easy to display during interactions with the employer. That is why it is imperative that you come to the interviews prepared and practiced. You want to be ready to answer and provide examples fluently. The employer will definitely take notice if you are fumbling over your words and responses. Remember bad impressions are harder to recover from. The employer is also searching for individuals who are a good fit for their team environment, organization and who can succeed in the required workload. If you are serious about increasing your salary offer, you need to dig deeper.

During the interview process you want to gain the employer's trust and respect. You want hiring managers to identify you as a great fit on their team and see you as the solution to the challenges they are facing. The goal is to ask qualifying questions that will help you understand how you can fill that void for the employer and be a great asset to the company. Sometimes the employer doesn't really understand what they are lacking; they just need someone as soon as possible to fill a position and lighten the workload. Construct valuable open-ended questions, so you can identify the employer's challenges and needs. Be an excellent listener. Listening to understand, not to respond, is key. When you understand the employer's challenges and needs it will be easier for you to deliver your attributes as a solution. The objective is to draw the employer in to the point they demand you to be on their team. So, when you present your compensation request the employer will to be more willing to grant it.

Consider asking the following probing questions. *How long has this position been vacant? What were the biggest challenges for the previous employee in this role? How long was the previous employee in this role? What are the daily demands? What are the short- and long-term goals for the new hire?* Once you understand the needs, wants and demands of the role this is an opportunity to present your success stories. Highlight your achievements with your previous employer in similar situations that the new employer is currently facing. Develop relatability in your ability to resolve the challenges if extended the opportunity to join the team. Give the employer just enough to see you as an asset. Some women are very modest and shy away from shining the light on their achievements. This is not the time to be modest. It is essential to confidently create that vision for the employer that there is no other candidate best fit for that specific role but you. You have to provide supporting examples of prior employment successes. Be ready to incorporate your value, talent and assets to fill that employer's need.

There are several methods to deliver examples of your achievements. A frequently used method is the STAR method. STAR is the acronym for situation, task, action and result. STAR works by describing a situation that resulted in a positive outcome, the tasks involved in the situation, actions that were taken to complete the task and finally the results that were achieved due to the core of actions.

An example of the STAR method is as following.

Situation: The new hire employee retention turnover had dropped dramatically over 30 percent within a 2 year period.

Task: My goal was to generate new ideas and incentives that would result in a 15 percent increase of employee retention.

Action: I designed an employee engagement program with a volunteer board of employees to manage group activities, events and entertainment during lunch and afterhours.

Result: Within an 8-month duration we saw an 18 percent average increase in employee retention for new hires.

Highlighting your attributes is not just about recognizing your professional integrity, it is also about displaying your personality traits that can give you an edge over candidates with similar qualifications. Displaying your great personality could be your winning factor. Yes, employers want to be sure that you qualify for the position, but they also want to make sure you are a good fit for the culture of the organization. If you have obtained multiple jobs in your field with different employers, you know no one employer runs their business the exact same as another. The foundation and structure may be similar, but the operations and software are normally managed differently. With that being said, employers can train any qualifying employee to do the job how they see fit, but they cannot teach personality. Embrace your unique characteristics that positively separate you from the masses and help you shine.

Personality traits are challenging to validate on a resume, so it is critical to highlight them during the interview process. Share stories that exhibit how you perform in challenging, demanding, stressful and time-sensitive situations. If you know that you struggle in certain situations, it's time to create a solution. Don't give up. Use that self-awareness and share the strategies you are incorporating for improvement. Never end a conversation negatively. Always find a way to refocus the conversation on your positive attributes. Don't forget to remain upbeat and maintain an optimistic mindset. Stay in control of your nonverbal conversation.

NEGOTIATING WITH FINESSE

Salary negotiation is one of the many important conversations you cannot avoid having. To achieve financial advancement in a timely manner, salary negotiation is required. Your salary will never naturally catch up to the market if you do not negotiate. The objective before engaging in salary negotiation is to build confidence and obtain comfort, which will make your debate more credible.

The employer will actively listen to your request and justification. Confidence is developed through knowledge of your industry, awareness of your value and understanding of your competitive advantage in the market. Comfort is built with practice. Never underestimate the quality of preparation. Be ready with your negotiation points and redirecting techniques. Practice frequently with different scenarios. Keep in mind that salary negotiation is not about you versus them. You don't have to dominate the conversation to be a successful negotiator. Being an exceptional listener allows you to really comprehend what the employer wants, which empowers you to find a resolution that works for you both. The objective should be to display an attitude of WIN/WIN concerning the employer and yourself. This will give the hiring managers the impression that you are as concerned with their success as your own. Discussions should focus on what you are offering the employer, not on how the position will advance your career. You want the employer to feel that you are adamant about finding common ground. Your personal goal is to get the best salary possible, but you never want the employer to feel that is your only focus. Be assertive and exhibit enthusiasm throughout the entire interviewing process.

Remember to let the employer broach the topic of salary. You've practiced, researched and built up your confidence for this moment.

You could begin your counteroffer structure in the form of a question, asking if the salary is negotiable. Inquire if there is anything more they can do in terms of the salary. Depending on your level of comfort, this tactic might work for you. A direct response would be *how much do you think my experience and education is worth to this organization?* Another response could be, *I am gracious for the offer, however given the results I've achieved in my career, education and considering the competitive market, I would like to explore a higher compensation package.* You can also ask the employer for pay equity according to work and current experience. Your approach to salary negotiation depends on your level of comfort. Everyone is different, so choose the best fit for you. Just negotiate!

If the employer is adamant about you providing a number, apply the knowledge you obtained in your research. Keep your energy high and be unforgettable even if you lose control of the direction of the conversation. Avoid being confrontational or fidgety. Maintain self-control. Give a small range of 10 thousand dollars. Your bottom salary number should be the minimum amount you are willing to accept. Don't wait for the employer to ask you to justify your request. Provide support immediately following your salary request figure. Highlight all the contributions you helped previous employers achieve. Highlight your dedication to projects and assignments. Highlight your professional characteristics of being pro-active, dependable and your knowledge of the industry. Highlight values and behaviors that believe are assets to the company. Be optimistic. Always negotiate from a point of your professional strengths and overall significance you will bring to the organization. Plead your case, then stop talking. Don't drag on the debate longer than necessary. Give the hiring managers time to analyze the information and develop their thoughts.

Some women perceive silence as a negative and uncomfortable break in the conversation during salary negotiation. This theory is quite the opposite. A break in communication allows the other person to process the information that was delivered to them. Embrace the awkward silence. The employer's silence should be observed as a natural reaction to digesting the information received. Give them the opportunity to formulate a response to your request. Don't try to fill the silence with pointless statements; this will only result in the perception that you lack confidence in your request. Don't discredit yourself. You don't want to sabotage everything you worked so hard to achieve in your salary negotiation preparation. Fight the urge. Sit quietly, confidently and wait for the employer to respond.

The objective is to get a yes from the employer on all aspects of your compensation request, but that is not normally the case. Be mentally prepared for all possible responses. Be flexible. There is a possibility you could get a portion of your request. There is a possibility you could be completely rejected on all aspects. If the employer says no, it is not the end of the world. Don't take a no response personally. It's about finding the best fit for the company and finding the best fit for your life balance. You want great a compensation package for your labor, talents, experience and education. The employer wants a great employee who will provide results above and beyond expectations. Use your problem-solving. Take your time. Ask the employer for clarification if needed. Sway the employer to focus on your value and the asset you would be to the company. Resort to your prioritized list you created. Express alternative solutions to increasing the salary offer. Don't over exhaust the negotiation conversation. Know when it's time to stop negotiating and decide to accept or decline the job offer.

WHEN TO ACCEPT OR DECLINE A SALARY OFFER

At this point you've likely deployed all the salary negotiation tactics set forth in the previous chapters. You have displayed confidence in your worth, and you completed your due diligence of analysis of the market value of your education and experience within your desired region. It is presumed you incorporated negotiation tactics for the complete compensation package including monetary and nonmonetary benefits. You are now at the portion of the interviewing process where the employer offers you a job. You now have to evaluate the official offer based on your needs and wants that you itemized in your plan before the interview.

Remain realistic, logical and in control of your emotions.

Realize there is a chance you are not going to get all the bells and whistles in the final offer. However, per your negotiation process with the employer you should have an idea on the weighed factors the employer was willing to consider. Resort back to your plan and evaluate what you are willing to compromise. Ultimately the decision to accept or decline a job offer is yours. Considering your financial status of emergency will play a significant facture in whether you accept or decline a job offer. If you are job searching before the need is urgent then you have more flexibility and a significant lead way over salary satisfaction. No matter what your situation is, remain professional and respectful.

In instances where accepting or rejecting an offer is

difficult, request time to consider the offer. You can ask for a few days to make a final decision, expressing that you would like to evaluate the offer further. Ask them how soon they need your response. Maintain the same enthusiasm and gratitude for the offer. Most employers will allow 24 to 48 hours to receive your response. It is not necessary to use the full time extended to you by the employer. Properly weigh the pros and cons of the job offer and deliver a timely response.

When deciding to accept or decline a job offer, refer to your strategy of preparation. What was your initial plan? How well does the job offer line up with your needs, wants and life balance? How does the job offer address your prioritized list? How far are you from getting what you need or want? Do you have other offers or interviews to consider? You must be honest and realistic with yourself. Is the market working in your favor? Is your profession in demand right now? Some specialized professions are only in demand seasonally. Do you have the prospects to wait for a better job proposal? Understand your why. Why are you looking for new employment? Is it to advance your career? Are you currently unemployed? Is your current employer downsizing? Are you tired of your current employer? Understand your options.

The obvious reason to accept is if you hit a home run and are offered the complete package, which means you are all ready to set a start date. If the job offer met all your prioritized needs, there is no reason to decline unless you are waiting to receive an offer from another equally desired employer. In this case, I would suggest requesting additional time to consider the first offer. Notify the employer with the pending job offer of your first official offer.

This way if the pending employer is serious about bringing you on the team, they will expedite the job offer, and it could work in your favor. Let the employer with the pending offer know that you want to make an informed decision on all options available. If you were able to successfully win over the employer, they will make a more desirable offer. Remain humble, enthusiastic and genuine to all potential employers.

Warning! Whatever job you decide to accept, do not burn your bridges with other. Show gratitude for the opportunity, consideration and experience. You want to leave the employer with a positive lasting impression of you. Never want to sabotage a relationship with a hiring manager even if you decline the offer. This will immediately cancel any counteroffer opportunities the employer might have considered offering you. If you are able to make an unforgettable and lasting impression on the employer, they will be willing to work harder to get you on their team. The employer cannot help but to acknowledge you for maintaining your class and professional status even in delivering an undesirable notice to decline employment. If the employers are sincerely fascinated by your personality traits and qualifications, they may refer you for another position within the organization that meets your salary requirements. Another reason why you should maintain your enthusiasm and gratitude is you never know when you will cross paths again in your journey of life. The person conducting the interview could be a future employer for another company, client, resource, associate, neighbor or child's teacher; you get the point.

When accepting a new position with a new

employer, you always want to remain professional with your existing employer. You never want to leave employment on bad terms. It's not worth it. Always give the professional two weeks' notice and show your gratitude for the opportunity to work with them. Even if the existing employer was terrible to you, not giving them two weeks' notice is not the best revenge. The best revenge is leaving gracefully and maintaining your dignity. This also secures you in the future, if you need to come back to that employer for work. Remember, even if that manager leaves your existing company, your exit interview remains in the company files.

EFFECTIVELY REQUEST FOR SALARY INCREASE

When requesting a salary increase there are advantages and disadvantages. If you are a good employee, you have already established a professional relationship and creditability with your employer. You understand the dynamics and culture of the organization and are familiar with the longevity and financial forecast of the company You should understand the management style of your boss before making the request. The disadvantage is the employer might take what you bring to the organization for granted. The employer could be oblivious to the workload you have accumulated over time. Most professional career responsibilities are not limited to their job description. It is up to you to make the employer aware of your value before the performance review and before requesting a salary increase. It is crucial to demonstrate to your employer when you have obtained additional responsibilities on real-time bases. This should not be conveyed as a negative but more a positive "for your information" conversation. Specific details of your accomplishments and acknowledgements received are essential to share with your employer. If you don't take the time to keep your employer well informed on your success, this can easily be an oversight by your manager. This is setting the foundation for your performance appraisal or salary negotiation meeting.

Requesting a salary increase from your current employer includes similar strategies as salary negotiation with a new employer. Before entering any discussion of salary with your manager, you must be prepared. Be familiar with the company policy regarding compensation. Some employers are restricted to annual salary increases due to budget limitations, while other employers may not have an annual salary increase set schedule. Most employers with annual salary increases are determined by performance appraisal with the opportunity to obtain up to a 5 percent salary increase. The merits are broken down by how many employees can achieve each percent level. Your objective is to maximize opportunity to achieve the maximum percentage available.

Have a clear indication of what you want to establish before the meeting. Are you solely seeking a salary increase or do you also want promotional opportunities? What are your flexibility points? Are you willing to negotiate more vacation days, weekly teleworking days or other benefits? Know your end goal. If you don't get a salary increase, promotion or any benefits incentives, are you willing to walk away from the job? Make sure you carefully weigh your options before you make that decision. You don't want to give an "or else" impression. Controlling your emotions is vital. Remember your nonverbal language is much louder than your verbal in most circumstances. You don't want to create unnecessary grief or cause the employer to be resentful.

Conduct your research on the salary range for your responsibilities, experience, education and job title. When doing your research don't limit yourself to online research, talk to your peers that you have developed a rapport within the organization. Don't directly ask what their salary is, but get their opinions on an acceptable salary range for the similar roles. Join professional networking or mentoring groups in your field. Be an active listener to gain the knowledge of the current market. Collect all your recent performance appraisals, awards, acknowledgements and professional development class certificates that are relevant to display that you are a great asset to the company.

Practice your approach, delivery and adversities your manger may demonstrate during the meeting. Practice your responses to anticipated questions from your manager. Rehearse in the mirror or with a friend. You want to take this conversation as serious as you would if you were interviewing for a new job. The manager's responsibility is still to conduct business in the best interest of the employer.

Once you have completing all your steps and are ready to talk to your manager about your salary, schedule the meeting. Identify your manager's style of management. Is your manger more receptive to a direct approach or does he or she have a more comfortable open-door policy? If your manager is more receptive to a direct approach, disclose exactly what you are hoping to accomplish in the meeting. If your manager has a comfortable open-door policy, then a general meeting request will probably suffice.

During the actual meeting with your manager, you want to demonstrate confidence, emotional control and belief that you deserve what you are requesting. Share with your manager your career goals within the organization, even if you don't plan to retire from there. You want to demonstrate your loyalty. Your manager will then consider the decision as an investment because your dialogue demonstrates longevity with the organization. Make sure your justification for a salary increase is not focused on excessive personal expenses but solely supported by what you bring to the organization. Embellish your contributions, project completions, enhancement trainings, certification completions. Share stories of your proactive track record at the organization. Don't take it for granted that your manager is keeping track of everything you have accomplished. Normally, high achieving employees are overlooked because the manager doesn't have to micromanage them. By providing good results, you are not on your manager's radar. Yes, it may get frustrating, but avoid being confrontational. Stay focused on your goals and what you practiced. Be assertive, confident and know your value. Highlight the values and behaviors you plan to incorporate for your employer. Don't lie, because like a child, your manager will remember all your promises. You always want to end the conversation on your professional strengths and not where you need to make improvements. If the discussion makes a turn toward your weakness, wait for the manager to finish then bring the conversation back to the values you are providing to the organization.

If you get a yes from your employer, you should anticipant an increase in your responsibilities. You are accountable for maintaining the satisfactory level that you utilized to convey your justification for a raise. If you get a no from your employer on all counts of your salary and benefits request, don't distress. Even if the manager abruptly shut your request down, don't give up. If the manager provided you with an extensive reason of why a raise is not an option, do not conclude the meeting. It is up to you to redirect the resolution to the manager. No matter how the manager delivers the no response. Ask open-ended questions such as the following, "What are the metrics in determining a salary increase?" What are your recommendations to improve my current role? Ask for detailed goals that will have a direct effect on your salary.

Message from Author

I challenge you today and going forward to stop leaving money on the table for employers to slip back into their pockets! You now have the strategic tools to be properly compensated for your talent, hard work and value you bring to an organization.

Salary negotiation doesn't just affect your current living situation, it also predicts your future livelihood. How comfortable you will be in retirement is determined by the foundation you set with implementing salary negotiation and how well you manage your money.

Reclaim the thousands of dollars you left on the table in your previous years. Learn from your mistakes and grow from life's lessons. When you start expecting more, you will naturally work toward receiving more. Stop settling for less than you deserve in life. When you are negotiating, approach the discussion as if you were representing a high-profile client and your commission was on the line. You must believe in your worth. Remove doubt from your thoughts and embrace the strong, independent, ambitious woman you are!

Ms. Maya Angelou said it best with my favorite quote. "Do the best you can until you know better. Then when you know better, do better."
I hope now that you know better, you will now do better!

www.ingramcontent.com/pod-product-compliance
Lightning Source LLC
Chambersburg PA
CBHW032209040426
42449CB00005B/515